5 SECONDS OF SUMMER

By Marie Morreale

Children's Press®
An Imprint of Scholastic Inc.

Photographs ©: cover: KCR/Rex USA; back cover: Kevin Winter/
Getty Images; 1: Kevin Mazur/WireImage/Getty Images; 2
top: David Livingston/Getty Images; 2 bottom: Jason LaVeris/
FilmMagic/Getty Images; 3 left: Chance Yeh/FilmMagic/Getty
Images; 3 right: Gregg DeGuire/WireImage/Getty Images; 4-5
background: Wenn US Alamy Images; 5 inset top: Michael Tran/
FilmMagic/Getty Images; 5 inset center top: Kobby Dagan/
Shutterstock, Inc.; 5 inset center bottom, 5 inset bottom: Ethan
Miller/Getty Images; 7: David Livingston/Getty Images; 8: Ethan
Miller/Getty Images; 9 top left: Christie Goodwin/Redferns/
Getty Images; 9 top right: Anna Kucherova/Dreamstime; 9 bot-
tom left: Tero Hakala/Shutterstock, Inc.; 9 bottom right: Brendan
Hunter/iStockphoto; 11: Taylor Hill/FilmMagic/Getty Images; 12:
Kevin Mazur/WireImage/Getty Images; 13 top: Iakov Filimonov/
Shutterstock, Inc.; 13 center left: Jon Kopaloff/FilmMagic/Getty
Images; 13 center right: meral yildirim/iStockphoto; 13 bot-
tom: Alenavlad/Dreamstime; 15: Chance Yeh/FilmMagic/Getty
Images; 16: Ethan Miller/Getty Images; 17 top left: Lyaschedko/
Dreamstime; 17 top right: Gilbert Carrasquillo/GC Images/Getty
Images; 17 bottom: pioneer111/iStockphoto; 19: Gregg DeGuire/
WireImage/Getty Images; 20: Jeff Kravitz/FilmMagic/Getty Images;
21 top: Edurivero/Dreamstime; 21 center: DFree/Shutterstock,
Inc.; 21 bottom: Film Fanatic/Alamy Images; 22: Cindy Ord/Getty
Images for SiriusXM; 24: Jeff Kravitz/OneD/Getty Images; 25:
Kevin Winter/Getty Images; 26: CF imageSPACE/Splash News/
Newscom; 27 top: Shirlaine Forrest/WireImage/Getty Images;
27 bottom: Christopher Polk/Getty Images for MTV; 28: Steve
Jennings/WireImage/Getty Images; 30: Chance Yeh/FilmMagic/
Getty Images; 32: Tim Mosenfelder/Getty Images; 33: Kevin
Mazur/OneD/Getty Images; 34: Chelsea Lauren/WireImage/
Getty Images; 35: Myrna Suarez/Getty Images; 36: Michael Gray/
Dreamstime; 37 top: Etiennevoss/Dreamstime; 37 bottom left:
Lobur Alexey Ivanovich/Shutterstock, Inc.; 37 bottom right:
Gabrieldome/Dreamstime; 38 top: Stephen Lovekin/Getty Images;
38 center: Kobby Dagan/Shutterstock, Inc.; 38 bottom: Jaguar
PS/Shutterstock, Inc.; 39: Matt Baron/BEImages/Rex USA; 40:
Gustavo Caballero/Getty Images; 41: Ryan Pierse/Getty Images;
42: Douglas Gorenstein/NBC/NBCU Photo Bank via Getty Images;
45: Herjeby Jonas/Aftonbladet/IBL/Zuma Press.

Library of Congress Cataloging-in-Publication Data
Morreale, Marie.
  5 Seconds of Summer / by Marie Morreale.
    pages cm. — (Real bios)
  Includes bibliographical references and index.
  ISBN 978-0-531-21557-9 (library binding : alk. paper) — ISBN 978-
  0-531-21662-0 (pbk. : alk. paper)
  1. 5 Seconds of Summer (Musical group)—Juvenile literature. 2.
  Rock musicians—Australia—Biography—Juvenile literature. I.
  Title.
  ML3930.A12M67 2015
  782.42166092'2—dc23 [B]   2015008960

All rights reserved. Published in 2016 by Children's Press, an
imprint of Scholastic Inc.
Printed in the United States 113

SCHOLASTIC, CHILDREN'S PRESS, and associated logos are
trademarks and/or registered trademarks of Scholastic Inc.

1 2 3 4 5 6 7 8 9 10 R 25 24 23 22 21 20 19 18 17 16

5SOS's Luke, Michael, Ashton, and Calum are today's hottest band!

MEET 5 SECONDS OF SUMMER

Their official name is 5 Seconds of Summer, but their millions of fans know them as "5SOS" or "5sauce." To music lovers around the world, these awesome Aussies— Luke Hemmings, Michael Clifford, Ashton Irwin, and Calum Hood—are fantastic, fearsome, fantabulous stars.

Unless you've been living on top of the tallest mountain in the world or in a deep, dark cave, you have probably heard the basic story behind the 5SOS phenomenon. But when you check out this 5SOS *Real Bio*, you are going to learn so much more! Did you know that Luke loves to eat and eat and eat? Or that Michael wants to learn to play the flute? That Luke's mom once taught math to Ashton? That Calum has a dinosaur toothbrush? Check out hundreds of 5SOS facts, photos, lists, and quotes. Once you have, you'll be an awesomesauce A+ fan!

CONTENTS

Meet 5 Seconds
of Summer 3

CHAPTER ONE
Music Guys 6

CHAPTER TWO
Success! 22

CHAPTER THREE
Q&A 28

CHAPTER FOUR
Bits & Pieces 36

CHAPTER FIVE
What's Next? 42

Resources 46
Glossary 46
Index 47
About the Author 48

A 5SOS concert is a stand-up-and-cheer fest!

THE FANTASTIC 4

LUKE

CAPTAIN ENERGY

"I was a happy kid," Luke Hemmings wrote in the 5 Seconds of Summer official biography, *Hey, Let's Make a Band!* "We lived in a small town called Freemans Reach and I came from a small family—just me, Mum, Dad, and my two older brothers, Ben and Jack."

There was always music in the Hemmings's house. Luke's parents, Andrew and Liz, had a large record collection, and their youngest son often found himself poring over their "oldies but goodies." He was immediately drawn to rock bands such as Good Charlotte and Blink-182. At one time, Ben had fooled around with the guitar, so when Luke showed interest, big bro stepped in and taught him some basics. Brother Jack played the drums, and sometimes the guys would "make noise together."

Besides music, Luke was interested in . . . well, everything! He wasn't quite out of control, but he did admit, "I was always getting in trouble for stupid things.

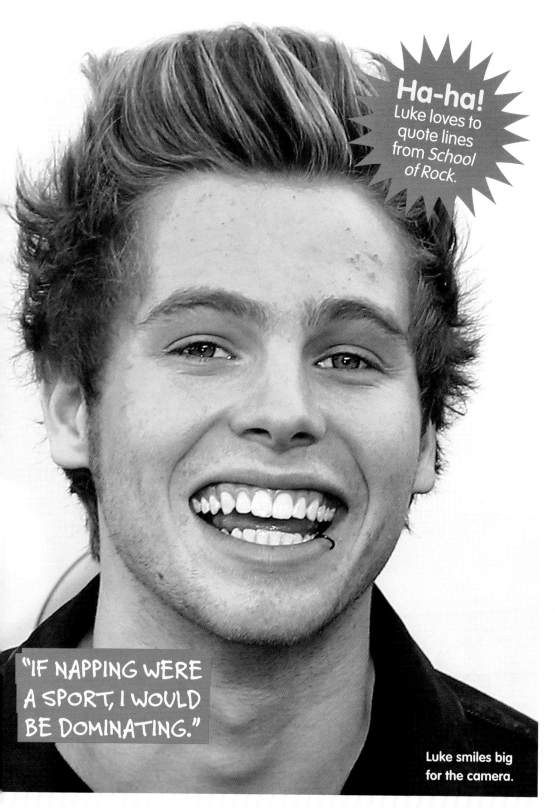

"IF NAPPING WERE A SPORT, I WOULD BE DOMINATING."

Luke smiles big for the camera.

At primary school I was in a world of my own and I often would get [in trouble] for being too loud. Then when I was around 6, I wouldn't go to class. I would be in school, but running around the playground having a great time while everyone else was in lessons."

By the time Luke was ready for high school, he had settled down a bit. However, his interest in music had only grown. He started attending Norwest Christian College in Year 7 (seventh grade) and was a bit of a loner because he was the new kid on the block. But music was always there for him. He took guitar lessons and watched tutorials on YouTube. He put his all into learning as much as he could. By Year 9 (ninth grade), he found himself sharing music classes at Norwest with Calum Hood and Michael Clifford. They realized they had the same bands on their playlists. This was the basis of their friendship.

Luke's YouTube videos were getting a good response, and when Michael saw a few of them, he had an idea. They had played together in class, so why not put together a band? YES!

There is nothing like being on-stage for Luke.

FACT FILE

IF LUKE WERE A CHICKEN, HE'D WANT TO BE COVERED WITH SAUCE FROM NANDO'S.

NAME: Luke Robert Hemmings

BIRTHPLACE: Sydney, Australia

PET: A dog named Molly

INSTRUMENT: Guitar

FIRST CONCERT ATTENDED: Good Charlotte

LUCKY NUMBER: Seven

FIRST YOUTUBE POST: He put up a video of himself singing solo on February 3, 2011

UNUSUAL TALENT: He ate 17 bowls of ice cream at once in an eating contest—he won

OUCH: His lower lip is pierced

TALLEST IN 5SOS: He is 6 feet 4 inches tall

KNOWN FOR: How much he can eat!

MUST-HAVE: He carries his hairbrush everywhere

FAVORITE ANIMAL: Penguin

FAVORITE SPORTS: Soccer, skateboarding, and snowboarding

FAVORITE BANDS: Blink-182, Green Day, Good Charlotte

FAVORITE COVER SONG: Katy Perry's "Teenage Dream"

FAVORITE SINGER/SONGWRITER/ PRODUCER: Pharrell Williams

FAVORITE PLACE TO RELAX: The beach

FAVORITE SUPERHERO: Batman

FAVORITE PASTIME: Napping

MICHAEL

WILD CHILD

Michael Clifford was born in Quakers Hill, near the city of Sydney. He is the only child of Karen and Daryl Clifford. Michael got his love of music from his dad, who plays the drums, but his real inspiration was the video game *Guitar Hero*. "Until that point, I hadn't really shown any musical talent," he wrote in *Hey, Let's Make a Band!* "I mainly sat in front of a computer screen and there's even a picture of me, aged about two, playing on a keyboard. I became quite an intense nerd. It's a miracle I didn't end up turning into some kind of a mad scientist."

Unfortunately, at the same time he was perfecting his guitar licks, his family was facing real trouble. "When I was about 12 or 13, life got a bit tougher for me because the **recession** happened and it hit Mum and Dad really hard," he revealed in *Hey, Let's Make a Band!*

Best Date
"A casual walk on the beach!"

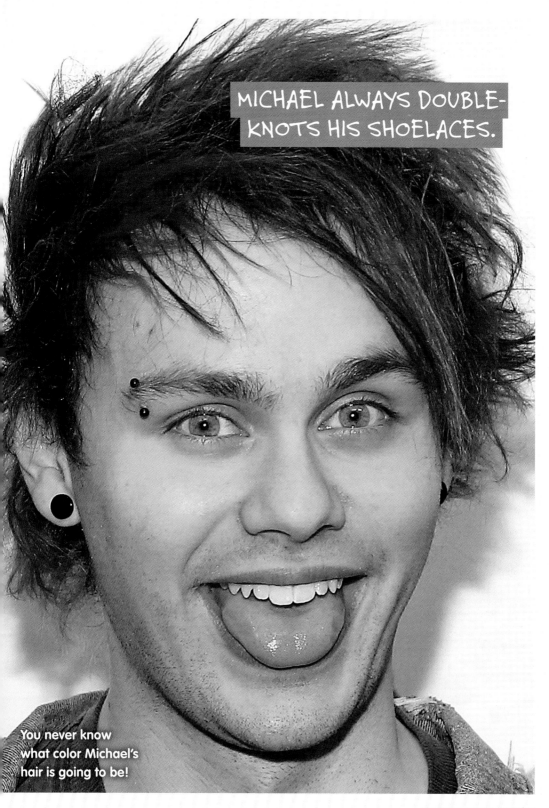

MICHAEL ALWAYS DOUBLE-KNOTS HIS SHOELACES.

You never know what color Michael's hair is going to be!

Michael is a guitar wizard!

Money was tight, and Michael saw his parents struggle to make ends meet. The experience made him realize he had to work hard for everything he got in life.

Michael's first real meeting with Luke and Calum came in music class. Soon they were staying after class and working on tunes of their own. Once they started putting up YouTube **covers** of their favorite artists, things seemed to fall in place.

Today, Michael is the first to urge newbies to the music business to put in the love, hours, and work to achieve their dreams. "We just started out playing covers on YouTube and it's kind of become a career," he told *Life Story* magazine. "I think it was just the fact being in a band means that you can have a career with three best friends. It just seemed like an amazing thing to do. But when we started it, we had no idea if we would be serious and actually be going on tour. To start a band, just work hard, appreciate everything that happens to you. It's hard to kind of answer this, because we were so lucky. Just, you know, work hard to get where you want to go and . . . um, be nice to people around you and practice. Yeah!"

FACT FILE

NAME: Michael Gordan Clifford

NICKNAME: Mikey

BIRTHPLACE: Sydney, Australia

PETS: A Siamese cat named Teddy and a poodle named Federer

MUSICAL IDOL: All Time Low's Alex Gaskarth

INSTRUMENT: Guitar

CELEB CRUSH: Ariana Grande

IDOLS: Jack Black, Bob Marley, and Bruno Mars

MUSICAL GOAL: To learn to play the flute

FAVORITE COLOR: Green

FAVORITE SUPERHERO: Spider-Man

FAVORITE ANIMALS: Whales and giraffes

FAVORITE BANDS: Led Zeppelin, Blink-182, All Time Low

FAVORITE DISNEY MOVIE: Frozen

FAVORITE MOVIE: Forrest Gump

FAVORITE CLOTHING: Plaid flannel shirts

FAVORITE WORD: Cheeseburger

FAVORITE TECH TOY: His iPhone

FAVORITE HATS: Snapbacks

FAVORITE VIDEO GAME: Destiny

WHEN MICHAEL WORKS OUT, HE WEARS BATMAN SHORTS—REALLY!

THE FANTASTIC 4
ASHTON

DRUMMER BOY

Born in the Sydney suburb of Hornsby, New South Wales, Ashton Irwin had a lot of responsibility very early on. "My parents split up when I was younger and being the oldest, I had to look after my sister. That was such a big thing to overcome," Ashton told *Top of the Pops* magazine. "My dad left, so growing up it was me, my mum and my younger sister—just the three of us until my younger brother came along. It can be scary and I think you've got to grow up a lot faster than you should sometimes."

Eventually the family settled in the small town of Richmond. Ashton's mom, Marie, encouraged her children to pursue the things they loved, so while in school, Ashton took acting classes, played soccer, and even began swimming competitively.

However, his longtime love was music. "I used to have a tape recorder and I would

2+2
Luke's mom, Liz, was Ashton's high school math teacher!

IF HE WEREN'T IN A BAND, ASHTON WOULD WANT TO BE A MUSIC TEACHER.

Ashton has a super collection of bandannas.

sit in my room and wait for my favorite songs to come on the radio," Ashton wrote in *Hey, Let's Make a Band!*

When Ashton was around eight years old, a friend asked him if he wanted to play the drums in a band. He said, YES! The only problem was he didn't actually know how to play the drums. Ashton's friend ended up teaching him some drum basics. He caught on quickly, and soon he was practicing every free minute of the day.

Ashton started playing the drums when he was eight.

Eventually, Ashton started playing with a diverse group of bands. In December 2011, Michael had set up 5 Seconds of Summer's first **gig**. As they practiced, the guys realized something was missing—a drummer! Michael remembered meeting Ashton at a party. He also remembered that Ashton was a good drummer, so he got on Facebook and sent him a message. "Hey, man, I don't know if you know our band, 5 Seconds of Summer, but we're doing this gig in the city soon—do you wanna play?" Michael recalled his note in *Hey, Let's Make a Band!* Minutes later, Michael got Ashton's response, "Yeah, man. I'd love to!"

Everything clicked, and 5SOS was born!

FACT FILE

NAME: Ashton Fletcher Irwin

NICKNAME: Ash

BIRTHPLACE: Hornsby, Australia

PET: A dog named Indie

HOBBY: Ice-skating

FIRST JOB: Behind the counter at KFC

FIRST BAND: Swallow the Goldfish

INSTRUMENTS: Drums, piano, guitar, saxophone

WORST HABIT: Forgetting his keys

NO-NO: Cats . . . he's allergic

FAVORITE COLOR: Red

FAVORITE ACTOR: Will Smith

FAVORITE MOVIE: The Pursuit of Happyness

Soundtrack of Life
"I need music to be me."

FAVORITE SINGERS: Jim Morrison and John Mayer

FAVORITE BAND: Coldplay

FAVORITE SPORTS: Soccer and swimming

FAVORITE PASTIME: Photography

FAVORITE TECH TOY: A Segway

FAVORITE SHOES: Vans

FAVORITE ANIMAL: Turtle

FAVORITE DISNEY MOVIE: Hercules

FAVORITE EXERCISE: Push-ups

ASHTON USED TO COACH A KIDS' SOCCER TEAM.

THE FANTASTIC 4
CALUM

SHY GUY

Calum Hood was born in a suburb just outside of Sydney. His parents, Joy and David Hood, both had demanding jobs. Calum was their second child. He has an older sister named Mali, with whom he is very close.

As a matter of fact, Calum credits Mali with encouraging his love of music. Mali sang in school productions, and at home Calum would listen to the R&B music coming out of her bedroom. He soon began to realize that music was in his heart. Things changed forever when he picked up a classical guitar that was lying around the house.

He started teaching himself to play guitar. Though he admits he tried several instruments without much success, the guitar was a perfect fit. It made him feel confident and happy.

Like Michael and Luke, Calum attended Norwest Christian College, but he wasn't as outgoing as they

Woof Woof!
"I just love dogs!"

"CALUM IS LIKE A CUDDLY LITTLE BEAR," SAYS ASHTON.

One reason Calum loves coming to America is the food!

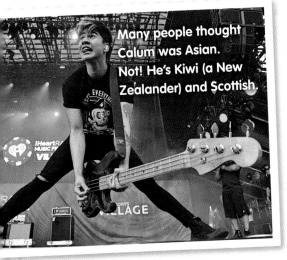
Many people thought Calum was Asian. Not! He's Kiwi (a New Zealander) and Scottish.

were. "I was a shy kid at school," he wrote in *Hey, Let's Make a Band!* "I never really spoke to anyone I didn't know or make too much eye contact. It took me a while to come out of my shell. . . . Despite my shyness back then, though, I made friends at school, but there were only a few close ones that knew a lot about me."

It was in music class that his relationship with Luke and Michael grew. Eventually, the guys decided to start a band. Turning down the name Bromance, they settled on Michael's suggestion, 5 Seconds of Summer. Whenever they could, they would get together and work on their sound and style.

Like any creative project, 5SOS was constantly growing and changing. They moved from doing R&B covers to more pop-punk covers. Then they moved from covers to original material. Ashton was invited to join the group as the drummer, and Calum switched from guitar to bass.

Little did he know that less than a year from then, 5SOS would be one of the best-known bands in the world.

5SOS ASKED FOR A DRESSING ROOM PUPPY AT THEIR CONCERTS, BUT CALUM SAYS, "WE NEVER GOT IT!"

FACT FILE

NAME: Calum Thomas Hood

BIRTHPLACE: Sydney, Australia

PET: A black mix-breed dog named Kuma

HOBBY/TALENT: Graffiti artist

INSTRUMENT: Bass guitar

CELEB CRUSHES: Alicia Keys, Katy Perry

FIRST KISS: When he was 13

FUN FACT: He has a dinosaur toothbrush

MUSICAL NOTE: Calum writes most of 5SOS's songs

MUSIC IDOLS: Green Day, Blink-182, Dave Grohl

DISLIKE: Salt and vinegar potato chips

FAVORITE SUPERPOWER: To be able to talk to animals

FAVORITE SPORT: Soccer

FAVORITE PRO SOCCER TEAM: Liverpool

FAVORITE COLOR: Blue

FAVORITE BIRD: Toucan

FAVORITE ANIMAL: Dog

FAVORITE ACTOR: Channing Tatum

FAVORITE CHILDHOOD MOVIE: Monsters, Inc.

FAVORITE MOVIE: The LEGO Movie

First Crush
Calum had a crush on Zoë Saldana when he was nine!

5SOS'S FIRST U.S. MINI TOUR SOLD OUT IN FIVE MINUTES!

When 5SOS was on a 2014 promo tour, they stopped in NYC's Sirius XM radio station for an interview.

5SOS...
MORE THAN A
NEW DIRECTION

THEY'RE NOT JUST A BOY BAND . . . THEY'RE SUPERSTARS!

The first indication of 5 Seconds of Summer's popularity came in 2011, when Luke, Calum, and Michael posted their cover of Chris Brown and Justin Bieber's "Next to You" on YouTube. The video received more than 600,000 hits. The threesome put in long hours of rehearsal, played gigs all over Sydney, and posted more videos on their YouTube channel. But something was missing. It was all about the beat. That problem was resolved when they added drummer Ashton Irwin to the mix. It was the start of something big. Success was calling, and the boys were ready to answer.

Dream On
Michael wants to be young forever.

5SOS opened for One Direction's 2014 *Where We Are* tour. Here they play the Rose Bowl in Cali.

WOW! Their Stars, Stripes, and Maple Syrup tour sold out in three minutes.

In 2012, 5SOS started posting original songs to their YouTube and gig playlists. They also released their first **EP**, *Unplugged*. In 2013, Calum and Luke wrote "Try Hard." It created a real buzz in Australia's music industry. Original songs like "Try Hard" won the band an opening slot for Hot Chelle Rae's 2012 Australian tour

5SOS's Timeline

Take Off with 5SOS

JULY 1, 2011
Calum, Michael, and Luke post a cover of "Next to You" on YouTube

DECEMBER 3, 2011
The first official 5SOS gig with Ashton is held

at Sydney's Annandale Hotel

JUNE 26, 2012
5SOS's first EP, *Unplugged*, is released

and a deal with Capitol Records. The buzz was getting louder. 5SOS fans started calling DJs, asking them to include the band on their playlists. Though there was a lot of hype surrounding 5SOS, the boys knew they had hard work ahead of them.

They improved their musical and writing skills, met people who could help them, and learned how committed they had to be if they wanted to make it. Then the biggest break of their career happened. One Direction asked 5SOS to open for their 2013 *Take Me Home* tour.

5SOS said yes to the tour, and not only did they get a career-making chance to play sold-out arenas with 1D, but they also made five BFFs. On top of that, Luke, Ashton, Calum, and Michael got to travel to places they had never been.

FEBRUARY 23, 2013
5SOS joins 1D's *Take Me Home* tour

MAY 18, 2014
5SOS performs at the *Billboard* Music Awards

MAY 23, 2014
5SOS opens for the European and North American legs of 1D's *Where We Are* tour

JULY 15, 2014
"Amnesia" is released and goes platinum

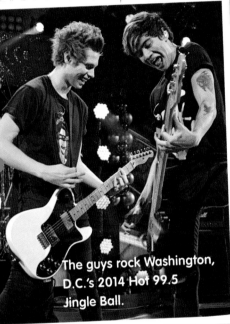

The guys rock Washington, D.C.'s 2014 Hot 99.5 Jingle Ball.

The year 2014 was a really big one for 5SOS. They began touring on their own, out of 1D's shadow. In April 2014, they also released their second EP, *She Looks So Perfect*, which debuted at number two on the *Billboard* 200 chart. In May, they released their mega-hit single "Don't Stop," and later that month they once again joined One Direction on tour. Also in July, 5SOS released their first full album, *5 Seconds of Summer*.

By 2015, 5SOS seemed to be everybody's favorite group. When they announced the dates for their first **headlining** gig, the *Rock Out with Your Socks Out* tour, fans

JULY 22, 2014
The *5 Seconds of Summer* album is released

JULY 30, 2014
The *5 Seconds of Summer* album debuts at number one on the *Billboard* charts

AUGUST 10, 2014
5SOS wins Teen Choice Awards for Breakout Group and Summer Music Star: Group

AUGUST 24, 2014
5SOS wins the MTV Music Video Award for Best Lyric Video for "Don't Stop"

DECEMBER 15, 2014
5SOS's first live album, *LiveSOS*, is released

Autograph time! 5SOS signs copies of *She Looks So Perfect* for Manchester, England, fans.

hit the box office like a hurricane. The entire tour was sold out almost as soon as tickets went on sale!

The past three years have flown by for Luke, Ashton, Calum, and Michael. They couldn't be happier, but the one thing that makes them the proudest is that they are still the same four guys from Sydney who said, "Hey, let's make a band!"

JANUARY 7, 2015
5SOS wins the People's Choice Award for Favorite Breakout Artist

MAY 4, 2015
The *Rock Out with Your Socks Out* tour kicks off in Europe

2015
5SOS starts their own record label, Hi or Hey Records, and releases their second studio album

WOO-HOO!
GOOD CHARLOTTE IS
WORKING WITH 5SOS
ON THEIR 2ND ALBUM!

Michael and Luke break
into a guitar riff that brings
the house down!

5SOS

QUICK CHAT!

WHEN THE LADS START TALKING, THEY JUST CAN'T STOP! WE LOVE THAT!

Want to find out some interesting stuff about Luke, Ashton, Calum, and Michael of 5SOS? Of course you do! Read on and you'll get their answers to questions about early jobs, pet peeves, and fashion sense, as well as their love of fans, family, and friends.

ASHTON

On how to succeed in show business . . . "Be original. Like, be yourself. I think people love real people. So it's really important that you, you know, stay true to what you love and what you do."

On the 5SOS book *Hey, Let's Make a Band!* . . . "We've always wanted to release a book, and I think this book's special to us just because it sort of tells the tale of how we began and everything. . . . I don't think that gets told too accurately too often. So, you know, it's a great thing that we're doing this."

On how you keep being successful . . . "You always need to remember you don't know everything. In this industry you learn new things every day. I think that's the best part, like, you learn [from] people you meet. You learn [from] live performances that could be better. And that's one of the main things for us actually."

On why he got fired from his job in a video store . . . "I'm the drummer, so I tap on the benches a lot and I like to lay down some fat beats whilst at work

Oops! Ashton confessed he doesn't wash his bandannas very often!

on the benches and I used to sing. . . . It was like the end of the day. I was screaming [this song]. [The manager] didn't like that so . . . she told me that was it. Hit the road Jack."

"I WANT TO MAKE MUSIC TO HELP PEOPLE." —ASHTON

On his signature bandanna . . . "I really like what it represents. It's more than just a fashion thing to me. It represents my inspirations. I look up to a lot of old-school drummers from the '70s, '80s, and '90s. [They used to] wear bandannas to signify they were rock."

MICHAEL

On how they stay grounded . . . "I think it's kind of like where we grew up and how we grew up. It wasn't like we were that privileged and stuff and so we learned to appreciate everything and everyone around us and stuff. And then when we got into doing this and stuff, I guess it never left us."

On how he started playing the guitar . . .
"*Guitar Hero* . . . I got really, really good at that and I was like, 'Wow, I could play real guitar.' And then I played real guitar and [played] so badly. I was like, 'This is nothing like *Guitar Hero*.' I almost quit, but I just kept going and stuck in there."

On a silly thing he did as a kid . . . "I wrote a girl a 10-page letter when I was 10. I was trying to be cute, but I didn't really know how to spell!"

On what annoys him . . . "Pointless arguments are my biggest pet peeve in the world!"

On the first songs he learned to play on the guitar . . . "The first song I learned from start to finish was that awful tune 'Ode to Joy'—you probably would have heard it at school. After that I got to play Led Zeppelin's 'Stairway to Heaven,' but really badly. Then came the basic rock classics, like Deep Purple's 'Smoke on the Water.' I drove everyone mad playing that, but it soon paid off and after a year of practicing, I got an electric guitar when I was 11 years old."

Michael has 13 different hair colors!

If Calum could play a superhero in a movie, it would be Spider-Man.

On what a fan could do to catch his attention . . .

"Fill my house with alligators, definitely. That would be awesome. I'd like that."

On when he realized the band was a global success . . .

"I remember we were touring—we were doing a headline tour around Australia—and in Adelaide we were having lunch and we had this piece of paper that was put in front of us telling us we were doing a world tour and listing all the venues, and it was just endless pieces of paper. Mind-blowing!"

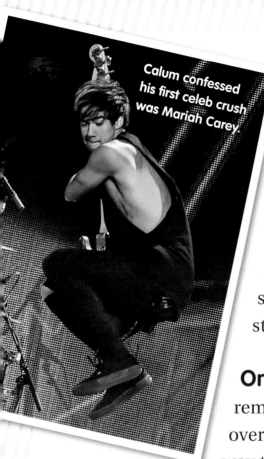

Calum confessed his first celeb crush was Mariah Carey.

On a little-known fact about him . . . "My nanna wanted to call me Robin!"

On how success has changed them . . . "A lot of things have changed in our lives, but we have remained the same kind of people we were. I still text my mom, like, every day."

On his love of music . . . "I remember the day when music took over my life: I was on the bus on the way to school and my sister's friend's brother handed me a burned CD with '*Green Day— American Idiot*' written on it with permanent marker. I put it in my CD player and literally could not stop listening to it. I loved everything about it: the angst, the rawness, the distorted guitars; it almost took me out of reality."

LUKE

On what makes him happiest . . . "I love it when a fan just comes up to tell us they are having the best time of their life."

On how to get their attention at a concert . . .

"I like big signs and funny signs. Or I see fans holding signs with Christmas lights wrapped around them. That definitely gets our attention!"

On how they pick a theme of a song . . .

"I think we try and write about our personal experiences. The only way to be original in your songwriting is to write about your own experiences, and I think that's what we try to do as a band."

On his worst date ever . . .

"I went on a date once where we went for sushi and I spilled soy sauce all over my plate and a little bit on her. I'm very clumsy when I'm nervous. I need a girl who can understand that!"

On not being popular in high school . . .

"We weren't too popular where we grew up when it came to girls. I was learning that at our school it was much better to be good at sports than be into music. The jocks were the popular kids; punks like us seemed a little odd to everyone."

Bet you didn't know . . . Luke owns four pairs of black skinny jeans!

5SOS TOP HITS

FOODIE FACTS, FUN STUFF, BFF QUOTES, & MORE!

FOODIE FUN

LUKE

QUICK MEAL: Pepperoni pizza
FAST FOOD: French fries
SNACK SPREAD: Nutella
SANDWICH: Ham and cheese
DINNER: Chicken or sushi
ICE CREAM: Cookies and cream
CANDY: Chocolate
FROZEN YOGURT SHOP: Pinkberry
RESTAURANT: Nando's

Down Under

In Australia, McDonald's is nicknamed Macca's.

MICHAEL

CANDY: Cadbury Twirl
FAST-FOOD RESTAURANTS: McDonald's and Nando's
MCDONALD'S ORDER: Cheeseburger with no onions or pickles, a Coke, a side of McNuggets, and sweet and sour sauce
QUICK MEAL: Pizza or baked beans
ETHNIC FOODS: Chinese and Indian
CHEWING GUM: Watermelon

ASHTON

FOOD: Spaghetti
DRINKS: Banana milkshakes and Lipton's Peach Iced Tea
SOUP: Chicken noodle
ICE CREAM: Chocolate chip
FRUIT: Pineapple
CANDY: Cadbury Caramello Koalas
SNACK: Pringles
HE COOKS: His specialties are barbecue and broccoli and rice

CALUM

FOOD: Pizza
PIZZA TOPPINGS: Ham and pineapple
ICE CREAM: Mint chocolate chip
DRINK: Tea
CHEESE: Cheddar
RESTAURANT: Nando's
BREAKFAST: Pancakes
FRUIT: Apples

Pringle-Man

Ashton admits he once ate a whole can!

CELEBRITY CHATTER ON 5SOS

Benji Madden: "5 Seconds of Summer remind me of Good Charlotte in the best possible way. They're younger than us. I'm glad they're doing this sound and I'm very happy to pass the torch. . . . We actually wrote 5SOS's song 'Amnesia' and it's [great] to see that sound coming back and being part of it."

Taylor Swift: Michael Clifford's sweet-tweet about Taylor's "Shake It Off" started a Twitter-patter. Tay Tay tweeted, "@Michael5SOS if I'm hearing you correctly, what you're saying is that you'd like to be twitter BFFs. I accept your implied request."

Bea Miller: During an interview with Ryan Seacrest, Bea jokingly asked, "Do you think if I ask [Luke Hemmings] to marry me, he'll feel really weirded out?" Ryan surprised her by getting Luke on the phone. He answered her question with, "I'd feel flattered. I'd probably say yes at the spur of the moment."

Ed Sheeran: "I think [5SOS are] really good. I think they've got great voices. I think the songs are good; I think their overall appeal is good."

Ariana Grande: "I think they're great. People are so crazy about them [and] their fans are so supportive and they're also very nice to my fans, so I'm grateful for that. They're really nice boys!"

MUST-KNOW DEETS

- Ashton would like to change his middle name, Fletcher, to Danger.
- The thing Ash misses most about Australia is the weather.
- Ashton loves cotton socks.
- Calum admits his worst habit is sleeping too much.
- Calum says that 5SOS fans are the best thing that has ever happened to him.
- Calum has an "innie" belly button.
- Luke admits that he was totally starstruck when he met Pharrell Williams.
- Luke's spirit cartoon character is a Ninja Turtle.
- Luke steals the other guys' underwear when he runs out of his own.
- Michael predicts that his last meal on earth would be pizza.
- The worst thing for Michael is having to get up early.
- Michael spends a whole day on his hair each time he changes its color.

BROMANCE

Some might think the friendship between 1D and 5SOS is a bit surprising. But when you hear them describe each other, you know they are true BFFs.

(L to R) 1D: Harry, Liam, Louis, and Niall

LUKE ON NIALL: After a visit to Niall's house, Luke enthused, "He actually has so much Coco Pops and chocolate cereal and it's just fantastic!"

NIALL TO ASHTON: Niall explained to Ashton why he likes hanging out with 5SOS: "Because you're my four other best friends and I love you."

LOUIS ON 5SOS: When the "Don't Stop" video premiered on TV, Louis tweeted, "New @5SOS video just come on the telly! Soooo proud of you boys!! Well done!"

LIAM ON 5SOS: "They are . . . great musicians. I am a bit jealous of them. I am working on learning to play [guitar] now, but I wish I had put the time in like they did when they were kids."

CALUM ON 1D: "There aren't too many pranks [with them on tour]—they have scary security guards. . . . There's usually a lot of fruit throwing though. They're really funny guys. Their humor is really similar to ours."

MICHAEL ON 1D: "They work hard!"

"WE WANT TO GO EVERYWHERE AND SEE AS MANY PEOPLE AS WE CAN."—CALUM

PERSONALITY TRAITS

LUKE . . . the shy one

ASHTON . . . the funny one

MICHAEL . . . the wild one

CALUM . . . the chill one

MUMS' BOYS

Check out 5SOS's Mother's Day tips . . .

MICHAEL: "When she says she doesn't want anything, she does."

CALUM: "If you make her breakfast, make sure you clean up afterwards."

ASHTON: "Don't ask her for money to buy her a gift. If you do, spend it all on her."

LUKE: "When she says she wants to hear from you, she doesn't mean on Facebook!"

5SOS: "The best thing you can give her is a hug."

"WE JUST DEMAND CUDDLES!"—MICHAEL

On their first appearance on *The Tonight Show Starring Jimmy Fallon*, 5SOS really rocked it!

5SOS ISN'T GOING TO STOP!

THE 4 AWESOME AUSSIES HAVE MORE TO CONQUER

During a 2014 interview with popscoop.org, Luke, Calum, Michael, and Ashton took a look back at the previous years. In typical 5SOS-speak, their responses were a bit random.

Ashton: "Where were we three years ago? I was working at a video shop."

Calum: "Like you think back and [you are] just like, 'Oh, it's crazy what can happen in such a short time.' We've worked like nonstop, so it's been a bit of a blur."

Luke: "Feels like more than two and a half years or three years."

Michael: "I can't actually remember not being in the band. . . . I can't remember anything before December 3, 2011 [laughter]. Everything's gone."

Actually, everything is ahead of them. 5SOS has hit all the high marks of a superstar musical career—awards, sold-out arena shows, worldwide fame, millions of die-hard fans, a huge social media following, and much more. The most amazing part is that they have remained true to who they are both musically and personally. Of course, they have grown and expanded their reach, but that's because they are creative superstars. Michael explained to *Billboard*, "We have definitely been influenced by punk and rock bands, but we're not ashamed to say that we want to get our music to as many people as possible."

And that fine-tuning of their talents makes for an unlimited future. While music is 5SOS's heart and soul, they realize there is more to it than performing, recording, and touring. That shows up in some of their goals. They have a vision for what might come next. For instance, Michael would love to bring 5SOS into the gaming world. "I would love for us to be in a video game," he told spin.com. "I'm a huge, huge, huge gamer. Avid . . . I would say, probably quite obsessed. If our song got on a video game, it would probably, instantly, become my favorite video game."

That's the fun side, but Luke, Michael, Calum, and Ashton have also learned a lot about business during their time in the music industry. That knowledge helped them create their own label, Hi or Hey Records. Luke told *Billboard* they wanted to sign "a girl version of us" and in 2015 they took on Hey Violet as their first artist. Hey Violet opened for 5SOS's *Rock Out with Your Socks Out* tour.

5SOS has had much success cowriting with some of the most popular artists around. They plan on continuing to reach out to other musical legends. Calum told the *Daily Star* that he and 1D's Niall have discussed writing together. "There're a few pop rock ideas kicking around already," he explained. "We'd love to make it happen."

By the time they released *5 Seconds of Summer*, the lads were already working on their next album. Ashton told pressparty.com, "I don't want to write the same album again, so I go out there and see what life has for me, and then I'll go back and I'll write about it."

"WHEN FANS TAKE THE TIME OUT OF THEIR DAY TO WRITE A LETTER, THAT'S REALLY SPECIAL TO US."—CALUM

That's how good songwriters work—they write about the things they have experienced. And you can bet that 5SOS has had lots of brand-new experiences, both good and

There is always something going on when the boys of 5SOS are together!

bad, since their early days. It's a growth process and it keeps a group relevant to more people. Right now, 5SOS's fans are mostly girls, but Michael explained one way 5SOS plans to expand their universe. "I think eventually we are going to evolve into being more accessible to dudes," he told thoughtcatalog.com. "As our fans grow up, so will our music. I think it's just a matter of time. . . . Hopefully we will see more dudes at the shows."

No matter how high their star rises, you can believe that one thing is not going to change about Luke, Ashton, Calum, and Michael. "We don't see ourselves [as famous]," Ashton told *Us* magazine. "We're just a band. But being in this band is the most wonderful thing ever. It's amazing to travel the world." Luke summed it up by adding, "It's just cool we get to do what we love. And people love that we do it!"

Resources

BOOKS

Croft, Malcolm. *5 Seconds of Summer: The Ultimate Fan Book.* Hauppauge, NY: Barron's, 2014.

5 Seconds of Summer. *Hey, Let's Make a Band! The Official 5SOS Book.* New York: HarperCollins Children's Books, 2014.

Williams, Imogen. *5 Seconds of Summer: 100% Unofficial.* New York: Aladdin, 2014.

Facts for Now

Visit this Scholastic Web site for more information on **5 Seconds of Summer:**
www.factsfornow.scholastic.com
Enter the keywords **5 Seconds of Summer**

Glossary

covers *(KUHV-urz)* versions of a song made popular by another performer

EP *(EE PEE)* short for "extended play"; an EP is shorter than a full album but longer than a single

gig *(GIG)* a live concert

headlining *(HED-lye-ning)* performing as the main artist at a concert

recession *(ri-SESH-uhn)* a time when business slows down and more workers than usual are unemployed

Index

American Idiot (Green Day), 34

"Amnesia" single, 25, 38

Annandale Hotel, 24

band name, 20

Bieber, Justin, 23

Billboard magazine, 26, 43, 44

Billboard Music Awards, 25

Brown, Chris, 23

Capitol Records, 25

Clifford, Michael, 8, 10, 12, 13, 16, 18, 20, 23, 24, 25, 27, 31–33, 37, 38, 39, 40, 41, 42, 43, 44, 45

"Don't Stop" single, 26, 40

Facebook, 16, 41

Fact Files
 Ashton Irwin, 17
 Calum Hood, 21
 Luke Hemmings, 9
 Michael Clifford, 13

fans, 25, 27, 33, 34, 35, 38, 39, 43, 44, 45

5 Seconds of Summer album, 26, 44

foods, 36–37, 39, 40

Good Charlotte, 6, 38

Grande, Ariana, 38

Green Day, 34

Guitar Hero video game, 10, 31

Hemmings, Luke, 6, 8, 9, 12, 14, 18, 20, 23, 24, 25, 27, 34–35, 36, 38, 39, 40, 41, 42, 43, 44, 45

Hey, Let's Make a Band! biography, 6, 10, 16, 20, 29–30

Hey Violet, 44

Hi or Hey Records, 27, 44

Hood, Calum, 8, 12, 18, 20, 21, 23, 24, 25, 27, 33–34, 37, 39, 40, 41, 42, 44, 45

Horan, Niall, 40, 44

Hot Chelle Rae, 24

Irwin, Ashton, 14, 16, 17, 20, 23, 24, 25, 27, 29–31, 37, 39, 40, 41, 42, 44, 45

Life Story magazine, 12

LiveSOS album, 26

Madden, Benji, 38

Miller, Bea, 38

Mother's Day tips, 41

MTV Music Video Awards, 26

"Next to You" (Chris Brown and Justin Bieber), 23, 24

Norwest Christian College, 8, 18, 20

One Direction, 25, 26, 40, 44

People's Choice Awards, 27

personality traits, 41

Rock Out with Your Socks Out tour, 26–27, 44

Saldana, Zoë, 21

Seacrest, Ryan, 38

"Shake It Off" (Taylor Swift), 38

Sheeran, Ed, 38

She Looks So Perfect EP, 26

social media, 16, 38, 40, 41, 43

songwriting, 20, 24, 25, 35, 38, 44–45

Stars, Stripes, and Maple Syrup tour, 24

Swift, Taylor, 38

Take Me Home tour, 25

Teen Choice Awards, 26

thoughtcatalog.com, 45

Tomlinson, Louis, 40

Top of the Pops magazine, 14

"Try Hard" single, 24

Twitter, 38, 40

Unplugged EP, 24

Us magazine, 45

video games, 10, 31, 43–44

videos, 8, 12, 23, 24, 26, 40

Where We Are tour, 25

Williams, Pharrell, 39

YouTube, 8, 12, 23, 24

Acknowledgments

Page 6: Luke—happy kid: *Hey! Let's Make A Band! The Official 5SOS Book*, October 2014; Luke—getting into trouble: *J-14*, January 2015
Page 7: Luke blurb: *People Collector's Special: All About 5 Seconds of Summer*, October 2014
Page 10: Michael's musical talent: *Hey! Let's Make A Band! The Official 5SOS Book*, October 2014; Michael and recession: *Hey! Let's Make A Band! The Official 5SOS Book*, October 2014
Page 12: Michael playing covers: *Life Story 5SOS Collector's Edition* 2014
Page 13: Bug Buggy burst: *People Collector's Special: All About 5 Seconds of Summer*, October 2014
Page 14: Ashton—parents' split: *Top of the Pops*, July 7, 2014; Ashton and tape recorder: *Hey! Let's Make A Band! The Official 5SOS Book*, October 2014
Page 16: Ashton—joining 5SOS: *Hey! Let's Make A Band! The Official 5SOS Book*, October 2014
Page 17: Soundtrack of Life burst: *People Collector's Special: All About 5 Seconds of Summer*, October 2014
Page 18: Woof Woof! burst: *Life Story 5SOS Collector's Edition* 2014
Page 19: Cuddly bear: *Life Story 5SOS Collector's Edition* 2014
Page 20: Calum—shy guy: *Hey! Let's Make A Band! The Official 5SOS Book*, October 2014
Page 25: Calum blurb: *J-14*, August 2014
Page 29: Ashton—show biz: YouTube; Ashton—5SOS book: YouTube
Page 30: Ashton—successful: popscoop.org March, 2, 2014; Ashton—video store: 5sosonline.com
Page 31: Ashton—bandanna: Seventeen.com 2014; Michael—grounded: popscoop.org March, 2, 2014; Michael—guitar: seventeen.com 2014
Page 32: Michael—as a kid: *Tiger Beat*, January/February 2015; Michael—pet peeve: *People Collector's Special: All About 5 Seconds of Summer*, October 2014; Michael—first songs: *Hey! Let's Make A Band! The Official 5SOS Book*, October 2014
Page 33: Calum—get his attention: *Tops of Pops*/unrealitytv.co.uk September 14, 2014; Calum—global success: *Life Story 5SOS Collector's Edition* 2014
Page 34: Calum—little known fact: *People Collector's Special: All About 5 Seconds of Summer*, October 2014; Calum—success: *People Collector's Special: All About 5 Seconds of Summer*, October 2014; Calum—love of music: *Hey! Let's Make A Band! The Official 5SOS Book*, October 2014; Luke—happiest: *Tiger Beat* March 2015
Page 35: Luke—attention at concert: *Tiger Beat* March 2015; Luke—theme of a song: Seventeen.com 2014; Luke—worst date: *Tiger Beat* January/February 2015; Luke—high school: *Hey! Let's Make A Band! The Official 5SOS Book*, October 2014
Page 38: Benji Madden: officialcharts.com September 15, 2014; Taylor Swift: Twitter/hollywoodlife.com December 2, 2014; Bea Miller: *On Air with Ryan Seacrest* November 5, 2014; Ed Sheeran: capitalFM.com; Ariana Grande: thehothits.com May 2014
Page 40: Luke on Niall: *J-14* September 2014; Niall to Ashton: *J-14* September 2014; Louis on 5SOS: Twitter/pressparty.com June 2, 2014; Liam on 5SOS: *Sunday Telegram*/*Daily Mail* May 2014; Calum on 1D: seventeen.com 2014; Michael on 1D: missoandfriends.com May 19, 2014; Calum blurb: *People Collector's Special: All About 5 Seconds of Summer*, October 2014
Page 41: Mums' boys: CapitalFM interview March 2014; Michael blurb: Radio 1 July 2014
Page 42: 5SOS chat: popscoop.org March 2, 2014
Page 43: Punk/rock: *Billboard* April 12, 2014; Video game: spin.com October 17, 2014; Luke blurb: *Unauthorized 5 Seconds of Summer Ultimate Fan Book* 2014
Page 44: Girl version of 5SOS: *Billboard* August 9, 2014; Write with Niall: capitalfm.com March 6, 2014; Not the same album: presspart.com August 21, 2014; Calum blurb: *Tiger Beat* March 2015
Page 45: Music evolves: thoughtcatalog.com August 18, 2014; Famous: *Us Special Collector's Edition: One Direction*, March 25, 2012

About the Author

Marie Morreale is the author of many official and unofficial celebrity biographies. She attended New York University as an English/creative writing major and began her writing and editorial career in New York City. As the editor of teen/music magazines *Teen Machine* and *Jam!*, she covered TV, film, and music personalities and interviewed superstars such as Michael Jackson, Britney Spears, and Justin Timberlake/*NSYNC. Morreale was also an editor/writer at Little Golden Books.

Today, she is the executive editor, Media, of Scholastic Classroom Magazines writing about pop-culture, sports, news, and special events. Morreale lives in New York City and is entertained daily by her two Maine coon cats, Cher and Sullivan.